EMMANUEL JOSEPH

Anti-dote for Job Termination

Copyright © 2025 by Emmanuel Joseph

All rights reserved. No part of this publication may be reproduced, stored or transmitted in any form or by any means, electronic, mechanical, photocopying, recording, scanning, or otherwise without written permission from the publisher. It is illegal to copy this book, post it to a website, or distribute it by any other means without permission.

First edition

This book was professionally typeset on Reedsy. Find out more at reedsy.com

Contents

1	Chapter 1	1
2	Chapter 1: Acknowledging the Emotional Impact	3
3	Chapter 2: Reassessing Your Financial Situation	5
4	Chapter 3: Reflecting on Your Career Path	7
5	Chapter 4: Updating Your Resume and Online Presence	8
6	Chapter 5: Navigating the Job Search Process	10
7	Chapter 6: Embracing Temporary or Freelance Work	11
8	Chapter 7: Focusing on Personal Growth	12
9	Chapter 8: Exploring Entrepreneurship	13
10	Chapter 9: Adapting to Remote Work	14
11	Chapter 10: Building Resilience	15
12	Chapter 11: Rebuilding Confidence	16
13	Chapter 12: Moving Forward with Purpose	17

Contents

1. Chapter 1 — 1
2. Chapter 1: Acknowledging the Emotional Impact — 3
3. Chapter 2: Reassessing Your Financial Situation — 5
4. Chapter 3: Reflecting on Your Career Path — 7
5. Chapter 4: Updating Your Resume and Online Presence — 8
6. Chapter 5: Navigating the Job Search Process — 10
7. Chapter 6: Embracing Temporary or Freelance Work — 11
8. Chapter 7: Focusing on Personal Growth — 12
9. Chapter 8: Exploring Entrepreneurship — 13
10. Chapter 9: Adapting to Remote Work — 14
11. Chapter 10: Building Resilience — 15
12. Chapter 11: Rebuilding Confidence — 16
13. Chapter 12: Moving Forward with Purpose — 17

1

Chapter 1

Introduction

Losing a job is one of life's most challenging experiences. It's not just about the financial instability it brings but also the emotional and psychological impact that often accompanies job termination. For many, a job is more than just a source of income; it represents security, identity, and purpose. When that is abruptly taken away, it can feel like the ground has shifted beneath you. But this book, "Recovering from Job Termination," aims to guide you through this turbulent period and help you emerge stronger and more resilient.

The initial shock of job termination can be overwhelming. It's natural to feel a whirlwind of emotions—confusion, anger, sadness, and even relief. The key is to acknowledge these feelings without letting them consume you. In the following chapters, we'll explore ways to process these emotions healthily and constructively. Remember, it's okay to grieve this loss, but it's also important to keep moving forward.

Financial concerns often top the list of worries after job termination. Without a steady paycheck, the future can seem uncertain and daunting. This book will provide practical advice on reassessing your financial situation, creating a budget, and exploring available resources to help you stay afloat during this transition. The goal is to empower you to take control of your finances, even in the face of uncertainty.

Beyond the immediate financial and emotional challenges, job termination offers a unique opportunity for self-reflection and growth. This period of transition can be a chance to evaluate your career path, identify your strengths and passions, and consider new opportunities. We'll delve into strategies for updating your resume, enhancing your online presence, and navigating the job market with renewed confidence.

Personal growth is a crucial aspect of recovering from job termination. It's an opportunity to develop new skills, pursue interests you previously didn't have time for, and build resilience. We'll discuss the importance of self-care, embracing a growth mindset, and setting achievable goals. This journey is about more than just finding a new job; it's about rediscovering your sense of purpose and direction.

Adapting to new ways of working, such as remote work or freelancing, is another topic we'll cover. These alternatives can provide flexibility and new opportunities you might not have considered before. We'll explore the dynamics of remote work, the potential of freelancing, and tips for successfully managing these options. Embracing change and being open to new possibilities is key to thriving in today's ever-evolving job market.

Building a support network is essential during this time. Surrounding yourself with friends, family, and mentors who can offer guidance and encouragement can make a significant difference. We'll discuss the importance of reaching out for support and staying connected with your professional network. You're not alone in this journey, and having a strong support system can help you stay motivated and focused.

Ultimately, "Recovering from Job Termination" is about turning a challenging experience into an opportunity for growth and new beginnings. It's about reclaiming your sense of self-worth, setting new goals, and moving forward with confidence and purpose. This book is your companion on this journey, offering practical advice, inspiration, and support every step of the way. Remember, job termination is not the end—it's the beginning of a new chapter filled with endless possibilities.

2

Chapter 1: Acknowledging the Emotional Impact

Facing the Initial Shock

The initial reaction to job termination often involves shock and disbelief. It's a natural response to an unexpected and life-altering event. Recognizing these emotions is the first step towards recovery.

Allowing Yourself to Grieve

Grieving the loss of your job is a vital process. It is important to allow yourself to feel sadness, anger, and frustration. These emotions are normal and part of the healing journey.

Seeking Support from Loved Ones

During this time, leaning on friends and family for emotional support can make a world of difference. Their empathy and encouragement can help you navigate this challenging period.

Embracing Self-Compassion

Practicing self-compassion involves treating yourself with kindness and understanding. Remind yourself that job termination does not define your worth or capabilities.

Considering Professional Help

If you find it difficult to cope with the emotional impact, seeking professional help from a therapist or counselor can provide valuable guidance and support.

3

Chapter 2: Reassessing Your Financial Situation

Reviewing Your Finances
Start by assessing your current financial status. Understanding your income, savings, and expenses will help you plan for the months ahead.

Creating a Budget
Develop a budget that prioritizes essential expenses and reduces non-essential spending. This will help you manage your finances more effectively during this transition period.

Exploring Financial Assistance
Look into available financial assistance programs, such as unemployment benefits, grants, or loans. These resources can provide temporary relief as you search for new employment.

Cutting Costs Wisely
Identify areas where you can cut costs without compromising your quality of life. Simple changes, such as reducing subscriptions or cooking at home, can make a significant difference.

Planning for the Future
While managing your current financial situation is crucial, also consider long-term financial planning. Set achievable goals to rebuild your financial

stability over time.

2

Chapter 1: Acknowledging the Emotional Impact

Facing the Initial Shock
The initial reaction to job termination often involves shock and disbelief. It's a natural response to an unexpected and life-altering event. Recognizing these emotions is the first step towards recovery.

Allowing Yourself to Grieve
Grieving the loss of your job is a vital process. It is important to allow yourself to feel sadness, anger, and frustration. These emotions are normal and part of the healing journey.

Seeking Support from Loved Ones
During this time, leaning on friends and family for emotional support can make a world of difference. Their empathy and encouragement can help you navigate this challenging period.

Embracing Self-Compassion
Practicing self-compassion involves treating yourself with kindness and understanding. Remind yourself that job termination does not define your worth or capabilities.

Considering Professional Help
If you find it difficult to cope with the emotional impact, seeking professional help from a therapist or counselor can provide valuable guidance and

support.

3

Chapter 2: Reassessing Your Financial Situation

Reviewing Your Finances
Start by assessing your current financial status. Understanding your income, savings, and expenses will help you plan for the months ahead.

Creating a Budget
Develop a budget that prioritizes essential expenses and reduces non-essential spending. This will help you manage your finances more effectively during this transition period.

Exploring Financial Assistance
Look into available financial assistance programs, such as unemployment benefits, grants, or loans. These resources can provide temporary relief as you search for new employment.

Cutting Costs Wisely
Identify areas where you can cut costs without compromising your quality of life. Simple changes, such as reducing subscriptions or cooking at home, can make a significant difference.

Planning for the Future
While managing your current financial situation is crucial, also consider long-term financial planning. Set achievable goals to rebuild your financial

stability over time.

4

Chapter 3: Reflecting on Your Career Path

Analyzing Past Experiences
Take time to reflect on your previous job experiences. Identify what you enjoyed, what you excelled at, and what you would prefer to avoid in the future.

Identifying Transferable Skills
Focus on the skills and knowledge you have acquired that can be applied to different roles or industries. Transferable skills are valuable assets in the job market.

Considering New Opportunities
Explore new career opportunities that align with your interests and strengths. This may be the perfect time to pursue a passion or change career paths altogether.

Seeking Professional Development
Invest in professional development by taking courses, attending workshops, or obtaining certifications. Continuous learning can enhance your employability and open new doors.

Setting Career Goals
Set clear, achievable career goals that reflect your aspirations and values. Having a roadmap will guide your job search and keep you motivated.

5

Chapter 4: Updating Your Resume and Online Presence

Refreshing Your Resume
Revise your resume to highlight your most recent experiences and accomplishments. Ensure it is tailored to the type of jobs you are seeking.

Crafting a Compelling Cover Letter
A well-crafted cover letter can make a strong first impression. Personalize it for each job application to demonstrate your genuine interest and fit for the role.

Optimizing Your LinkedIn Profile
Update your LinkedIn profile to reflect your current career objectives. Networking on LinkedIn can connect you with potential employers and industry professionals.

Building a Professional Portfolio
If applicable, create a portfolio showcasing your work. This is especially useful for creative fields where visual or written examples of your work can demonstrate your skills.

Seeking Recommendations
Reach out to former colleagues, supervisors, or clients for recommendations. Positive testimonials can enhance your credibility and attract

prospective employers.

6

Chapter 5: Navigating the Job Search Process

Researching Job Opportunities
Dedicate time to researching job opportunities that align with your skills and interests. Utilize job boards, company websites, and recruitment agencies.

Applying Strategically
Apply for positions that match your qualifications and career goals. Customize each application to show how your experience and skills meet the job requirements.

Networking Effectively
Networking is a powerful tool in the job search process. Attend industry events, join professional groups, and connect with people in your field.

Preparing for Interviews
Prepare for interviews by practicing common questions and developing compelling answers. Confidence and preparation are key to making a strong impression.

Staying Positive and Persistent
The job search can be challenging, but maintaining a positive attitude and staying persistent will increase your chances of success. Celebrate small wins along the way.

7

Chapter 6: Embracing Temporary or Freelance Work

Exploring Freelance Opportunities
Consider freelance work as a temporary solution or a potential long-term career path. Freelancing allows for flexibility and can help bridge financial gaps.

Taking on Temporary Roles

Temporary roles or contract positions can provide income and valuable experience. They also offer opportunities to network and possibly lead to permanent positions.

Diversifying Your Income Streams

Think about diversifying your income through multiple streams, such as part-time jobs, consulting, or starting a small business. This can provide financial stability and new opportunities.

Managing Freelance Work Effectively

If you choose to freelance, develop strategies to manage your workload, set boundaries, and maintain a healthy work-life balance.

Evaluating Long-Term Potential

Assess the long-term potential of temporary or freelance work. Determine if it aligns with your career goals and consider making it a permanent part of your career strategy.

8

Chapter 7: Focusing on Personal Growth

P ***rioritizing Self-Care***
Make self-care a priority during this transition. Engage in activities that promote physical, mental, and emotional well-being, such as exercise, meditation, and hobbies.

Developing New Skills

Use this time to develop new skills or pursue interests you previously did not have time for. Learning new things can boost your confidence and open new career possibilities.

Building a Support System

Surround yourself with a support system of friends, family, and mentors. Their encouragement and advice can be invaluable as you navigate this period of change.

Embracing a Growth Mindset

Adopt a growth mindset that views challenges as opportunities for learning and development. This positive outlook will help you stay motivated and resilient.

Celebrating Progress

Celebrate the progress you make, no matter how small. Recognizing your achievements will keep you motivated and remind you that you are moving forward.

9

Chapter 8: Exploring Entrepreneurship

Assessing Your Entrepreneurial Potential
Evaluate your interest in and readiness for entrepreneurship. Consider your strengths, weaknesses, and the resources available to you.

Identifying Business Ideas
Brainstorm business ideas that align with your skills, passions, and market needs. Conduct research to validate the viability of your ideas.

Creating a Business Plan
Develop a comprehensive business plan outlining your goals, strategies, and financial projections. A solid plan will guide your entrepreneurial journey.

Securing Funding
Explore funding options, such as personal savings, loans, grants, or investors. Ensure you have the financial resources needed to start and sustain your business.

Launching Your Business
Take the plunge and launch your business. Stay adaptable, continuously seek feedback, and be prepared to make adjustments as needed.

10

Chapter 9: Adapting to Remote Work

Understanding Remote Work Dynamics
Learn about the dynamics of remote work, including communication tools, collaboration methods, and time management strategies.

Setting Up a Home Office
Create a dedicated workspace that is conducive to productivity and free from distractions. Invest in the necessary equipment and maintain a professional work environment.

Establishing Work-Life Balance
Establish boundaries between work and personal life to maintain a healthy work-life balance. Set a schedule and stick to it to avoid burnout.

Enhancing Remote Communication Skills
Develop strong communication skills to stay connected with your team and clients. Effective communication is key to successful remote work.

Enhancing Remote Communication Skills (continued)
Enhancing remote communication skills involves using clear, concise, and effective communication methods to stay connected with your team and clients. Utilize video conferencing, instant messaging, and collaborative tools to maintain strong relationships and ensure smooth workflows.

11

Chapter 10: Building Resilience

Understanding Resilience

Resilience is the ability to bounce back from adversity. It's not about avoiding challenges but learning to adapt and thrive despite them. Recognize that building resilience is a gradual process that requires effort and patience.

Developing Coping Strategies

Identify and develop coping strategies that work for you. These may include mindfulness practices, physical exercise, creative outlets, or engaging in activities that bring you joy.

Learning from Setbacks

View setbacks as opportunities to learn and grow. Analyze what went wrong and what you can do differently in the future. This mindset will help you approach challenges with a positive outlook.

Cultivating a Support Network

Cultivate a support network of friends, family, and mentors who can offer guidance and encouragement. Sharing your experiences and receiving support can significantly boost your resilience.

Setting Realistic Goals

Set realistic goals that are achievable and aligned with your current circumstances. Breaking larger goals into smaller, manageable steps will help you stay focused and motivated.

12

Chapter 11: Rebuilding Confidence

Recognizing Your Achievements
Take time to recognize and celebrate your achievements, no matter how small. Acknowledging your successes will help rebuild your confidence and remind you of your capabilities.

Practicing Positive Self-Talk
Replace negative self-talk with positive affirmations. Remind yourself of your strengths, skills, and past accomplishments. This practice can boost your self-esteem and confidence.

Stepping Out of Your Comfort Zone
Challenge yourself to step out of your comfort zone and take on new experiences. Trying new things can help you grow and build confidence in your abilities.

Seeking Constructive Feedback
Seek constructive feedback from trusted sources to identify areas for improvement. Use this feedback to make positive changes and enhance your skills and performance.

Embracing a Growth Mindset
Adopt a growth mindset that views challenges as opportunities for development. Embrace the idea that you can continuously learn and improve, regardless of setbacks.

13

Chapter 12: Moving Forward with Purpose

Defining Your Purpose

Reflect on what gives your life and career purpose. Identify your core values, passions, and long-term aspirations. Understanding your purpose will guide your decisions and actions.

Setting Long-Term Goals

Set long-term goals that align with your purpose and vision for the future. Create a clear plan to achieve these goals, and stay committed to your path.

Embracing Change

Embrace change as an inevitable part of life. Be open to new opportunities and experiences, and view change as a chance to grow and evolve.

Practicing Gratitude

Practice gratitude by regularly acknowledging the positive aspects of your life. Gratitude can enhance your overall well-being and help you maintain a positive outlook.

Living Intentionally

Live intentionally by making conscious choices that align with your values and goals. Stay focused on what truly matters to you, and let your purpose guide your actions.

Book Description

"Recovering from Job Termination" is a heartfelt guide for anyone navigating the difficult aftermath of losing a job. It's more than just a manual on getting back into the workforce; it's a comprehensive journey of self-discovery, resilience, and transformation. This book offers practical advice and emotional support, helping readers to process their feelings, reassess their financial situation, and explore new career opportunities. It's about turning what seems like an end into a new beginning, full of possibilities and growth.

The book delves into the emotional rollercoaster that often follows job termination. From dealing with the initial shock and grief to building self-compassion and seeking support, it provides strategies to help readers heal and move forward. Financial stability is another crucial aspect, and the book offers detailed guidance on budgeting, exploring financial assistance, and planning for the future. By addressing these critical areas, "Recovering from Job Termination" ensures readers are well-equipped to handle the practical challenges that arise during this transition.

Ultimately, "Recovering from Job Termination" is about empowerment and personal growth. It encourages readers to reflect on their career paths, develop new skills, and embrace new opportunities, whether in traditional employment, freelance work, or entrepreneurship. The book emphasizes the importance of building resilience, maintaining a positive mindset, and living with purpose. With its compassionate tone and actionable advice, this book is a trusted companion for anyone looking to rebuild their confidence and create a fulfilling future after job loss.

www.ingramcontent.com/pod-product-compliance
Lightning Source LLC
LaVergne TN
LVHW020509080526
838202LV00057B/6256